Kansas City ROYALS

KENNY ABDO

Fly!
An Imprint of Abdo Zoom
abdobooks.com

abdobooks.com

Published by Abdo Zoom, a division of ABDO, P.O. Box 398166, Minneapolis, Minnesota 55439.

Printed in the United States of America, North Mankato, Minnesota.
102025
012026

Photo Credits: AP Images, Getty Images, Missouri State Archives, Shutterstock
Production Contributors: Kenny Abdo, Jennie Forsberg, Grace Hansen
Design Contributors: Candice Keimig, Neil Klinepier

Library of Congress Control Number: 2025936774

Publisher's Cataloging-in-Publication Data

Names: Abdo, Kenny, author.
Title: Kansas City Royals / by Kenny Abdo
Description: Minneapolis, Minnesota : Abdo Zoom, 2026 | Series: MLB teams | Includes online resources and index.
Identifiers: ISBN 9798384940203 (lib. bdg.) | ISBN 9798384940968 (ebook) | ISBN 9798384941347 (read-to-me ebook)
Subjects: LCSH: Kansas City Royals (Baseball team)--Juvenile literature. | Baseball teams--Juvenile literature. | Professional sports--Juvenile literature. | Sports franchises--Juvenile literature. | Major League Baseball (Organization)--Juvenile literature.
Classification: DDC 796.357--dc23

Table of CONTENTS

ROYALS

With four **pennants**, two World Series rings, and an army of fans at the ready, the Kansas City Royals are a team truly fit for a king!

KC
Royals

For almost 60 years, Kansas City has had a long line of baseball legends step up to help the Royals take their rightful throne!

BATTER UP!

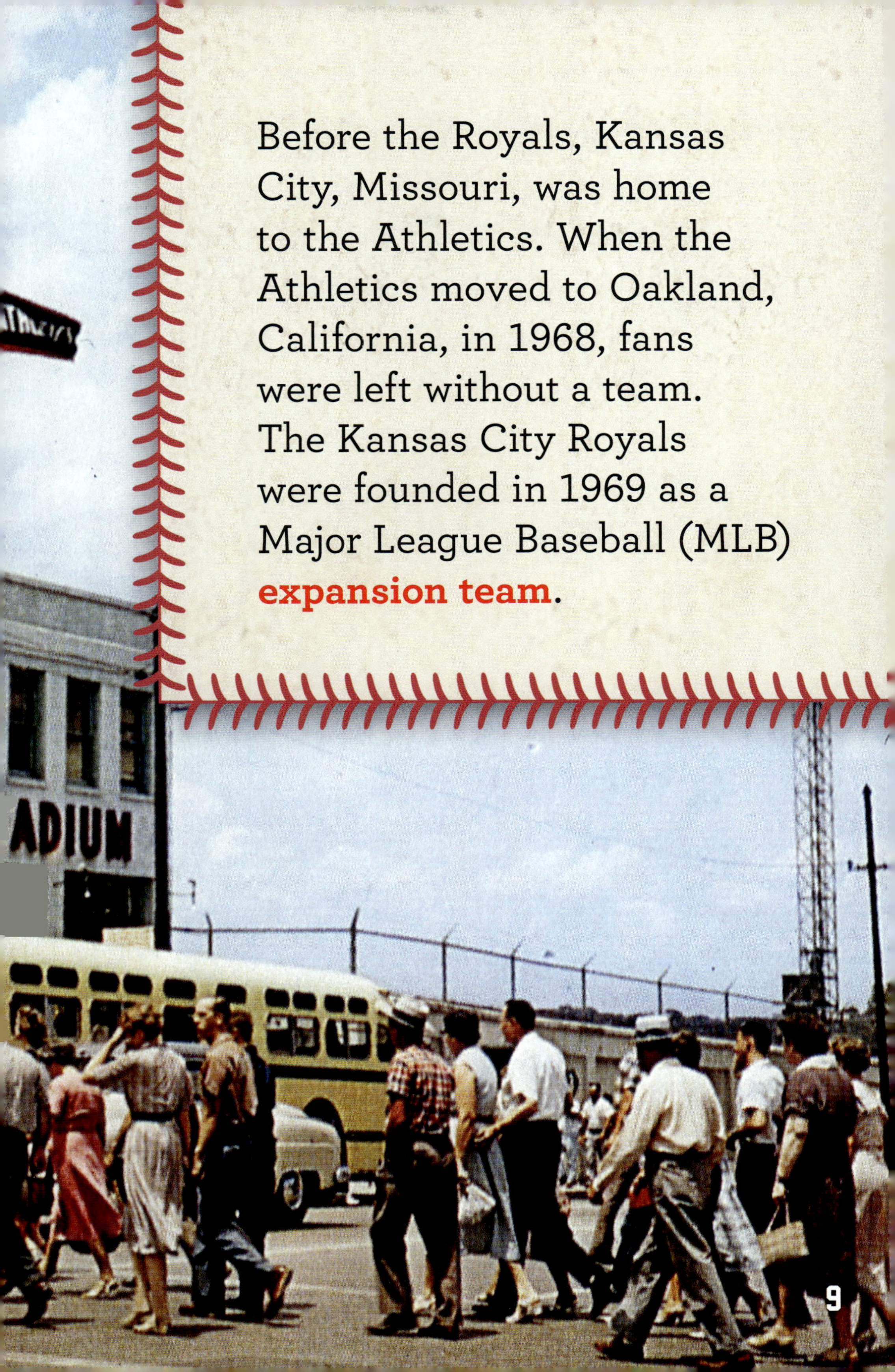

Before the Royals, Kansas City, Missouri, was home to the Athletics. When the Athletics moved to Oakland, California, in 1968, fans were left without a team. The Kansas City Royals were founded in 1969 as a Major League Baseball (MLB) **expansion team**.

The Royals played their first game on April 8, 1969, against the Twins. They lost 12–3, but the city had its team back. It was the beginning of a new chapter for Kansas City baseball.

From 1976 to 1978, the Royals won the **American League (AL)** West three years in a row. But each time, they lost to the Yankees in the playoffs. During that stretch, George Brett became one of the team's best hitters and a rising star in baseball.

KC
KANSAS

GRAND SLAMS

The Royals reached the World Series for the first time in 1980. They played against the Phillies but lost in six games. Despite the loss, it was a huge **milestone** for the young team.

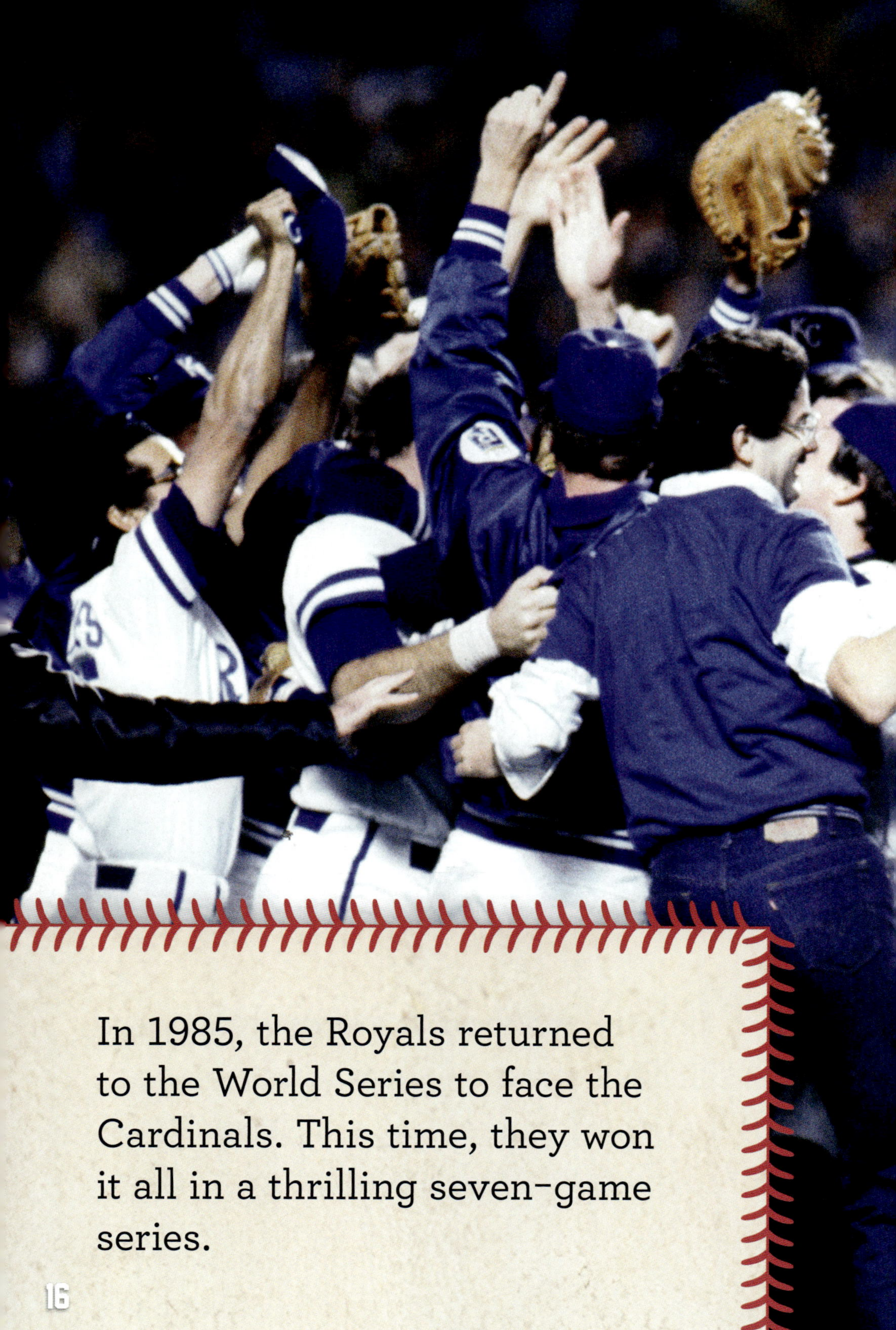

In 1985, the Royals returned to the World Series to face the Cardinals. This time, they won it all in a thrilling seven-game series.

The entire team played beautifully. But George Brett's game was exceptional. He finished the series with a .370 batting average, 10 hits, and 5 runs scored.

The Royals spent most of the 1990s with losing **records** and no playoff appearances. The team changed **managers** and players often, which made it hard to find a good groove. By the 2010s, the Royals began to rebuild with new talent and strong leadership.

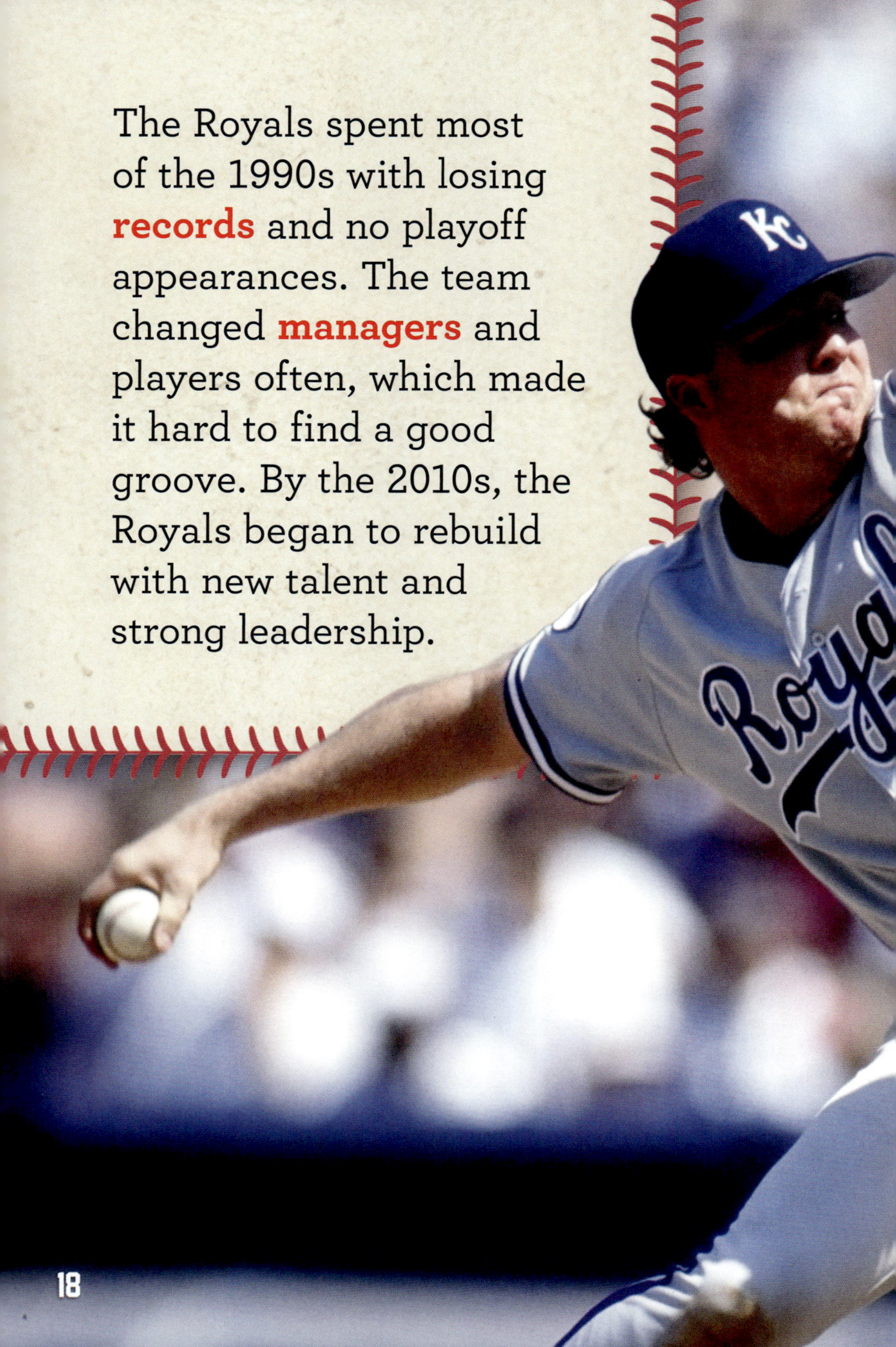

Royals
1
Royals
8
KC

Young stars like Eric Hosmer and Salvador Pérez helped the Royals reach the 2014 World Series. The team lost, but seemed to have found its stride. The next season, the Royals defeated the Mets in five games to win the 2015 World Series!

KC

In 2024, the Royals finished the regular season with a solid 86 wins. Cole Ragans struck out 223 batters before getting injured. Bobby Witt Jr. hit .332 with 32 home runs and 31 steals. In 2025, Kris Bubic earned his first **All-Star** selection and a 2.55 **ERA** before a season-ending injury. Still, fans could feel another strong season was soon to come.

HALL OF FAME

Frank White was a standout second baseman who spent 18 seasons with the Royals from 1973 to 1990. Known for his sharp defense and timely hitting, he helped lead the Royals to their 1985 World Series title. He was named to the Royals Hall of Fame in 1995.

KC
Royals
20
23

George Brett is a Royals icon who played his entire 21-season career with the team from 1973 to 1993. He won three batting titles, helped win the 1985 World Series, and collected over 3,000 hits and 1,596 **RBIs**. Brett was **inducted** into the Hall of Fame in 1999.

Salvador Pérez has been a Royals star since his **debut** in 2011. He has earned nine **All-Star** picks and helped win the 2015 World Series.

Pérez holds the team **record** for most home runs by a catcher and has earned praise for his leadership and clutch performances.

GLOSSARY

All-Star – an athlete named to the yearly baseball contest where top players from the AL and the National League (NL) compete against each other.

American League (AL) – one of two 15-team leagues that make up MLB.

debut – to perform in public for the first time.

Earned-Run Average (ERA) – the average number of earned runs per game scored against a pitcher.

expansion team – a new professional sports team added to an existing league.

inducted – brought in as a member.

manager – or field manager, the equivalent of a head coach who is responsible for overseeing and making final decisions.

milestone – an important event or turning point in a team's career.

pennant – the title achieved by the team that wins its division or league championship.

record – a team's season total of wins and losses; a top achievement by a player or team that no one has done before.

Runs Batted In (RBI) – a statistic that credits a batter for making a play that allows a run to be scored.

ONLINE RESOURCES

To learn more about the Kansas City Royals, please visit **abdobooklinks.com** or scan this QR code. These links are routinely monitored and updated to provide the most current information available.

INDEX